Benchwarmers

First published 2023 by The Hedgehog Poetry Press

Published in the UK by
The Hedgehog Poetry Press
5, Coppack House
Churchill Avenue
Clevedon
BS21 6QW

www.hedgehogpress.co.uk

ISBN: 978-1-913499-34-1

Copyright © Nigel Kent 2023

The right of Nigel Kent to be identified as the author of this work has been asserted in accordance with the Copyright, Designs and Patents Act 1988.

All rights reserved. No part of this publication may be reproduced, stored in or introduced into a retrieval system, or transmitted in any form, or by any means (electronic, mechanical, photocopying, recording or otherwise) without prior written permissions of the publisher. Any person who does any unauthorised act in relation to this publication may be liable for criminal prosecution and civil claims for damages.

9 8 7 6 5 4 3 2 1

A CIP Catalogue record for this book is available from the British Library.

Benchwarmers

by
Nigel Kent

For Kerry, Holly, Annie and Archie

Contents

The flight of the caged bird 8
Figured 10
Invisible Man 11
Waste 12
Graffiti 14
Benchwarmers 15
Damp 16
Spectrum 17
Pacemaker 18
Team Tantalus 19
He could've been a hero of a Thomas Hardy novel 20
Treadmill 22
Cut 23
The long run 24
Full chat* 26

Acknowledgements 28

THE FLIGHT OF THE CAGED BIRD

She arrives at the first
signs of summer:
a solitary migrant bird
fluttering through the door,
settling warily at a desk
by the window,
eyes fixed on the horizon
beyond the bars of the blinds.
Her untamed hair falls forward,
unable to curtain her
from the cruel curiosity
of the other kids
who prod and poke
with jibes as sharp
as whittled sticks.
I try to lure her
out with questions
but she's taken flight
into silence
where she glides
on warm thermals
over the village green,
where the caravan is parked,
to the nearby woods
where a feast of ink caps,
yolky chanterelles,
and wild garlic grows;
where loud foxgloves
and dog violets bark
for attention;
and where the trees

link their arms and sway
to a chorus of
of blackcaps, finches,
chiffchaffs and thrushes
singing of a time before
clipped wings and cages.

FIGURED

They surround me
in the playground,
push me to perform,
force-feed me calculations
like gamblers feed slots
in one-arm-bandits.

I send ribbons
of ticker tape answers
streaming into the air
far too fast
for them to grasp.

Tonight they will text
their mates about
the school's new curio -
'the weird kid,
quicker than a calculator.

They turned their backs
on numbers long ago;
they're blind to
the beauty of equations,
so delicately balanced,
deaf to the wisdom in formulae,
dead to the surging power of Ten.

They will never
know numbers like me.
I have my place
in their order
and friends in their fields.

INVISIBLE MAN

You passed me in the street today
without a flicker or a glance.
I was your classmate:
a silhouette in the shadows
of sun-bright memories.

I was the boy force-grown in the dark,
with the pale complexion,
who faded in the glow of attention
that made the rest of you shine,
the boy who ached for someone
to loosen the ties of shyness.

I was the one who sat alone,
in the double desk near the door,
audience to your banter
that bounced
from boy to boy to boy
but never in my direction.

How I wanted you
to throw me a word
that I could bat back,
even a sharp word
would have cut
a hole in the solitude
to pull me through,

but you never did
- you never did -
not then and not today.

WASTE

He keeps his anger
in the clenched fist
of a hand that has never
learned to use a pen
or held a parent's love,
the one he pounded
the pillow with each night
in every foster home
they've moved him to this year.

All day at school
the anger twists and turns,
pushing hard against
his fingertips that tremble
with the strain
of holding back,
but today his teacher
finds the words
to prise it loose.

It strips his knuckles
to the bone,
and leaves her lying
on the floor,
silenced.

Now racing down
the corridor he leaves
a trail of fear
that they follow
to his hiding place
beneath the waste
in a wheelie-bin
on the estate,
where his bloody fist
is clenched again.

The teacher's screamed
prophecy come true.

GRAFFITI

We are the pencil boys
not the posh propelling ones
but the shitty bookie's kind
you find on our estate.

We never bring pens to lessons
yet our teachers don't lend us theirs:
they think ink's too permanent
and pencil's easily rubbed out.

BENCHWARMERS

They live their lives in corridors
faces pressed against
the frosted glass of classroom doors.
The weary boys from the estate
who wear disaffection
like their team's strip.

The boys who lost life's toss
the moment they were born,
condemned to play a game
they know they'll never win,
always away from home
with rules they'll never master.

They are the own-goal-scorers
the penalty-kick-fluffers,
the red-carded-walkers,
the bottom-of-the-league boys,
relegation certainties
for this and every season.

DAMP

When our dad annoyed our mother,
which he did daily,
there was no flash of anger,
no sudden downpour,
but a steady drizzle
that soaked in seconds
and set in for days.
Even when we thought
her mood had improved,
the smell of damp lingered
in the living room walls.

SPECTRUM

When he was a child,
it was numbers alone
that would console him,
favoured, special numbers.

We'd watch him
scribble **9**
over and over again
on scraps of paper.
A forest of nines,
too dense for light or sound
to pierce its canopy.

Then there was **6,**
like the shape
of his special chair,
which he would turn
towards the wall's blankness
where with hands on knees
he'd rock away the hours,
and count each stitch
on shirt and jeans,
then start again.

Then there was **0,**
like the entrance to the cave
from which he couldn't be coaxed
and that none of us could enter.

PACEMAKER

He was a runner
before he learned to walk,
lurching, half-stumbling
at reckless speed towards
the river's rushing edge,
the concrete steps' abyss,
evading grasping hands,
deaf to his mother's gasps.

She bought him reins
to tame him, to train him
to walk caution's cushioned way
and though at first
he squirmed and strained
like a greyhound on a leash,
he learned at last to heed
her pull upon the lead.

Now a man, he lives his life
at walking pace, harnessed
still to a mother's will,
so after day has dawdled past
he drinks his malted milk,
and dozes by the fireside,
dreaming of the pinch of running shoes
and the slap of the open road.

TEAM TANTALUS

Game over, stadium empty,
anthems floating down the road,
a team of apprentices sent out
to clear the pitch of litter,
chase papers wafting
across the windswept grass
that feint one way,
then another, evading
their pleading hands,
like their hopes of selection
for next week's match.

HE COULD'VE BEEN A HERO OF A THOMAS HARDY NOVEL

If you beat
a dog long enough
and hard enough
you'll reveal the wolf within.

Fate certainly raised a stick
and brought it down
on our dad's back,
time and time again.

Yet when his mother died
before a year was out,
they say he cried no more
than any other child;

and when our mum berated
him for letting siblings
strip him of his legacy,
he didn't say a word;

and when she lost the girl
she'd longed for
and left the sting of grief
upon his cheek,
he slunk away unheard
to the silence of his shed;

and when returning home
he found the car
outside our house again,
the bedroom curtains closed,
he did not make a scene.

It wasn't until
we found his diary
and let loose
his muzzled thoughts
that we heard the snarl
uncurling from his throat.

TREADMILL

She doesn't look
at the lycra girls,
the nymphs of the gym,
sheathed in body confidence,
floating on pheromones,
and gently sculpting figures
that need no nip and tuck,
no silicone solutions,
just a simple pull and push
to mirror perfection.

She has eyes only for
the calorie counter,
hears only the voice
in her ear berating her,
feels only the flames
kindled in her calves,
burning in her belly,
flaring in her chest,
yet not melting her resolve
to win invisibility's race,
to experience the ecstasy
of evaporation
that leaves no stain behind,
not even on
the baggy tracksuit,
that crumples in a heap
on the treadmill's track,
spinning off with
arms outstretched
as if in celebration
of breaking the tape.

CUT

A prose poem

"I am what you designed me to be. I am your blade. You cannot now complain if you also feel the hurt." (Charles **Dickens**)

Their boy crosses the divide,   strays into the wastes of my estate,   where leather laptop bags, smart-arse phones and uni scarves   belittle and abuse.   At first his flesh resists, unyielding as the pulp of fruit   fallen too soon   from the tallest tree. I thrust again,   harder,   drop him to his knees,   rip open lips   in silent surprise, feel his tomorrows spill across my hand.   I leave my mark,   carve my initials in entitlement's bark   with the blade they made,   tempered with rejections, sharpened with their threat of sanctions. I'll take their cuts no longer,   I'm the one who makes them now.   I'm the headline hit-man,   the media sensation, yesterday's reject,   today's 'Most Wanted'.

THE LONG RUN

You pull me from
the comfort of my chair.
'Park, grandad!' you yell,
"Come on!"

Grumbling limbs
reluctantly agree,
though I cannot
run beside you
as you'd like me to.

I must take your hand
and be your brake instead,
the foot dragging on the ground
to slow you down.

Your hand will twist
and turn, struggle to be free,
but I'm your boundary,
the rope you cannot cross,
that holds you back
from the precipice of steps
protects you from
the concrete's smack.

Yet my grip is weak
and you're growing
stronger by the day.

Sometime soon, I know
that you'll break loose,
run off ahead,
much too fast for me
and I will shuffle after you,
following vainly your fading
footsteps up the road
till darkness falls

hoping you'll find
your own way home,

alone.

FULL CHAT*

He wasn't like
his former mates
from the estate
who customised
their speech
to 'piss off' parents
and pull the girls
with 'inits' and 'isits',
'dreds' and 'bluds'
'jams' and 'fams'.
He favoured vintage,
employed the model
passed down to him,
dedicated himself
to knowing its components,
to learning how they work,
to fuelling it from second-hand
classics and textbooks,
in anticipation of that moment
- that precious moment -
when for the first time
he would open up the throttle,
feel the surge of power,
and speed away
not looking back.

biker slang for describing the loud sound of a motorcycle full throttle.

ACKNOWLEDGEMENTS

With thanks to the editors of the publications and websites in which versions of some of these poems first appeared: *Blue Orange* and *Noises from the Isle,* Dreich; *#PoeticMapofReading Project,* The Southwark Libraries; *Poetry Non-stop,* Patrick Widdess; *Anger,* Paper Swan Press; *Impspired Magazine Volume 4;* Openings *38 and 39,* Open University Poets;

to Josephine Lay for her helpful editing and to Josephine again, Patricia M Osborne, Paul Brookes and Phil Vernon for their testimonials;

to Robin Evans, John Prangnell, Stephen Belinfante, Mike Dowling, Nick Browne, the Society of Open University Poets and the Hedgehog Poetry Community for their continuing support;

and finally, to Mark Davidson. Ironically for a poet, I cannot find the words to express my gratitude for the enthusiasm and commitment he has shown to my work over the last five years. A simple 'thank you' can never be enough.

www.ingramcontent.com/pod-product-compliance
Lightning Source LLC
Chambersburg PA
CBHW020141130526
44590CB00041B/622